sunny.

Gabrielle Hickmon

everything,
is a peace of a poem…

if
you're paying attention.

MELODIES

Devotion

"Whatcha writin bout?," he asked.
You, I thought.

I said "life," instead.

"You okay?" he was persistent tonight.
Face scrunched, pen in lip, allegory forming,
I answered, "Yea, I'm thinking."

Is this what safety feels like?

--

This is a book about all the "I love you's" I swallowed.
All the "I see you's" I only dared to communicate with
my eyes. The "I feel you's" wrapped up in skin-to-skin
contact I'm not even sure they felt.

It's a love letter to everyone I've loved and everyone I've
left; but maybe, really just one person in particular.

sunny, because it rained the day we met.
sunny, because it is the prelude to what was our foreplay.
sunny, because this project has been my saving grace in a
time where things have felt very dark.

sunny, because sun in window of church of you may
always be my favorite way to wake up.

"Whatcha writin bout?," he asked.
"You – but really me, we, us together,
or apart.," I answered.

Life has taught me, the sun is always the answer.

--

I fell in love in the fall in a window sill,
above a basement that was occasionally light filled.

I wrote this for, to, because, in spite of you and me,
rarely, sometimes, mostly never,
but always on Tuesday's 'we.'

I love you –
even though you've never been sure how you feel about
me.

--

sunny.

sunny.

**to everyone, but especially the girls
everywhere –
chasing the sun.**

naked.

i want to bear my soul to you,
bear the love I have for you – to you.
strip myself down to marrow and sinew,
leave all my cards on the table
and say
"Here I am."

i want to love you that way.
wholly myself.
holy self,
holy you,
holy love –
holy communion.

spirit to spirit.
flesh to flesh.
I want to love you without getting caught up in all of the
mess.

caught up in you,
caught up in me.
you, me, and love –
us three.

i want to love you in confident 'we's.'
plans I'm not worried you'll break
and texts I'm not afraid to send.

i want to love all of you
that loves all of me.
oh who am I kidding?
i already do.

to wear love on my arms and not put on a jacket.

i want to love you unhinged.

un-hinge, you.
unhinge for me,

would you?

naked.
from the intestines.

working on it.

working on it,
a work in progress,
haven't we learned we're all in process?

process,
progress,
provision –
are those the necessary steps?

steps for getting older,
steps for growing,
steps in life, love, and all that other good shit.

working on it,
"Do the work."
what does that even mean?
should I be pushing, pulling, or putting back together at
the seams?

seams...
seems like we're not getting anywhere,
seems like I should have left you there,
seems like there's something about you
that I just can't shake.

is that what the work is?
working to make this,
you, me, we, us, together,
great – again?
which, is to say it ever was.
was it?

working on it,
working at it.
"You check in? Know what's going on?
When?"

when was the last time you let yourself feel everything?
gave yourself over to the love,
the fear,
the soul of it all?

the souls of black folk.
the soul of this black folk.
the soul of me sees the soul of you,
and it never takes much working at it,
working on it –
for those two.

working at it,
working on it.
there is nothing wrong with you.
"I don't wanna do that to you."
so don't,
do 'that.'
whatever that is.

see I could get with this,
or I could get with that,
but please know
I will always choose you.

working at it,
working on it.
I'm working on me too.

working on, for, to, through, because, in spite of us —
together,
or apart.

working at it,
working on it.

"what I do? lol
and, you know I'm working on it."

The Parkway.

which address should I put down?
yours,
mine,
or ours?
hours.

hours spent in the church of you,
on my knees conversing with the king.
sending praises up,
legs coming down –
supplying *all* of my needs.

Warshan Shire taught me not to make homes out of
human beings…
no one said anything about making them with one
though.

in one though.
or rather,
you
in
me
though.

the way you'd stay inside,
long after we both came and went,
showed me
there's love in the lingering
and lust in the staying,
but heaven and home in the stealing away.

from behind the ear.

sunny.

worth.

you're not intimidating to those who are wo

whoknows.

i wanted flowers.
rose petals to be exact.
a room lit only by candles.
candle light.
lite.
lit.
I wanted to transcend light.

instead,
I got huffs and puffs,
house blowing down.
a rushed encounter,
t-shirts still on.

not sure I consented.
at least not to that.
no savoring,
no treasuring,
no "giving away."

moment I wanted so long to love someone for wrapped
up in pain.

i cried.
then,
still gave my soul away.

                    from underneath the tongue.

basements.

how does your neck fit so perfectly in mine?
too perfectly.
a perfect I couldn't,
didn't know how to trust.

neck that felt made for the crook in mine and breaths that
felt more intimate than a forehead kiss.
breaths that meant you felt safe,
in the crook of my neck,
adjacent to my arms,
nestled behind me.

hand just small enough to hold,
but big enough to grip me up.
be felt,
always.

wingspan long enough to envelope me and lengthy
enough to cover me when it rained.

that basement was my safe place.
shelter.

get-a-way from it all.
where breadth met depth and I felt seen,
heard,
valued,
and respected in every direction.

that,
I did stay in his track pants all day and reflect on how I
got this lucky kind of like.

difference being,
he was there too.
nestled,
in the crook of my neck.

legs entangled.
eyelashes fluttering.
breathing deep.
intertwined.
no one daring to move.

both of us unsure of what,
if anything
comes next
and wondering how the hell we got here so quickly.
yet safe,
and unwilling to leave the world we created together –
in the crook of my neck.

an ode to whole days spent in basements.

entangled.

it.

it was wet,
he was grey,
I was wind through trees –
soft.

stop.

it was waves,
fire,
hi(gh),

stop.

it was laughter and trying to make sense of it all,

stop.

falling into dark light,
beckoning me to him and him to into me,

stop.

twilight.
face next to mine
breath
hand on thigh,

stop.
stop.
stop.

entangled –
when shit escalates quickly.

t-shirts.

i donated all your t-shirts today…
finally gave away all the stuff you gave me.
stuff I took.
stuff I got tired of looking at.
reminders of the love,
memories of the loss,
the emotion of it all.

i donated all your t-shirts today…
one of many steps I've taken in attempts to purge my soul
of you.
purge my skin of you.
purge my mind of you.
purge me of you.
purge me from you.

i donated all your t-shirts today…
Jesus be a cut soul tie,
stopped up heart,
tear ducts with no tears,
gash with no bleeding,
cracked soul put back together again.

i donated all your t-shirts today…
coulda gave em back,
but that's not my style
and you're not,
never were an Indian giver.

more like,
we gave too much
but kept too little.

ᴜved too hard,
but didn't fight for the right things.

cared way more than enough,
but couldn't find the words to say so.

i donated all your t-shirts today...
all except the one that's way too big for both of us
but somehow fits me just right.

you used to fit me just right too
ya know.
remember?

i donated all your t-shirts today.

prototypes.

the taste of me lingers on his lips and
presence around.
know that someone,
I,
for better or worse was there –
before,
you.

his family still asks about me.
"How's XYZ?"
my family stopped asking a long time ago.

it's a holiday.
"Merry Christmas."
"Happy Birthday."
telling me this as if we didn't stop celebrating together
many, many moons ago.

you can see me in his eyes.
feel the warmth of my body on his skin.
come to know the things I taught him,
his light bulb moments
every time he opens his mouth to speak.

i am fire.
stand too close and you get burned.
he was water,
always trying to put me out.

maybe,
you two together
are sun and moon

yin and
day

yang
and night.

opposites that attract instead of extinguish.

at some point,
it becomes less about proving how happy you are without
the person and more about just being happy in your new
state of being.
it's not possible to "win the breakup."
sure, she isn't you, but maybe she is what he needs.
things you couldn't be.
what's wrong with that?

you don't care when you no longer have to proclaim that
sentiment.

caring is loud.
indifference is quiet.
and prototypes,
well,
they can change.
right?

sunny.

lane(lame).

trips down memory lane aren't worth the heart pains.

$$$.

"always have a stash
of mad
money,
to get you
on
the
road."

-   mom

green.

i hope your soil turns green again.

the way we were.

i think the last time I fully relaxed with a man was you –
the you there was,
the way we were before you broke my heart.

the me I was before I learned
forever don't last always.
all ways.

us together was safe until it wasn't.
you were home until you weren't.

i used to wear my heart on my sleeve.
can't find her anymore though.

                                        from the metro.

greens, beans, potatoes, tomatoes.

i think I measure love by how much I do or don't want to
write about you –
how often you show up in my work.

i feel most comfortable loving and living through the
written word,
loving and living in my head where I know what the
demons are
even if,
I am sometimes powerless to stop them.

stop them from negative self-talk.
stop them from spiraling a normal feeling into a
depressive one.
stop them from picking apart moments in search of a
story instead of just standing tall in them,
standing still in them,
standing them in good stead.

i noticed I do that when I'm with you too.
pick out pieces of our moments to see if poems are
hiding in them.
weaving words and worlds behind my eyes and always
within my hands.
stepping on stage and telling our story before it is time or
finished.

you make me want to live in the moment and love you
there,
outside of my head,
and better than on paper.
living in the real world with you –

that's what love looks like.

from the heart and behind the eyes.

a conjuring, a picture.

i wish I had taken a picture.

they say they're worth a thousand words,
but I only needed one.
wanted to cement the feeling I felt with you,
walking city streets,
arm in chest,
wording all along the way.

cement peace,
cement pieces,
cement being able to be
or say
or do.

you gave me an extra squeeze when you hugged me
goodbye –
I know
you knew
I'd notice.
I've taken it to mean
'thank you.'

you thanking me,
me thanking you.
for seeing me in a way that doesn't feel invasive,
for capturing my essence solely with your irises.

i wish I had taken a picture,
I'd like to meet the girl you see,

and see her,

ough your eyes.

from a walk that left me full.

to be continued…

this is how you lose me.
how you lost me.
how you never had me to begin with.

untitled.

when's the first time they showed up in your work?

intimacy is.

perpendicular legs
the church of you.
temples.
you end,
I begin,
we become us –
together.

time never hinders where we left off.
left,
leaving.
love,
lust,
lingering.
learning to let me,
you,
we,
be.

it's okay to be happy.
if only for a minute.
fleeting joy of body that feels like habit not needing
breaking.
no pretenses.

intimacy is me writing this poem
his game,
the space those exist in without question.
seeing your way through dark room.
curve of arm bent as shelter from road.
hand on contours and curves.

peace that says,
"We're okay,"
no matter what the world has to say.

finger rubbing thigh ever so lightly.
holly
go
lightly.
felt without feeling,
never
moving.

giddy,
quiet,
chilling.

a place past comfort.

                                                    seen.

sunny.

on.

i wonder who you tell about your days now?

riddle me this.

questions,
I leave them everywhere.

skype calls from Michigan to DC,
a kitchen nook in Lemington,
pillows in Philadelphia.
texts I never send,
calls I never place.

it's not that answers evade me,
it's that too many questions form.

"Are you cheating on me?"
"Do you love me too?"
"What were [have we been] for you?"

--

"I have a question."
"Might have an answer."

**why has my love never been what those I offered it to
wanted?
never been good enough?**

--

"Here you go again with the deep ass questions and shit."

loud.

you taught me how to bite my tongue.
I've never been this quiet.

memories.

i wish someone had told me the people we love and those
we're just with don't leave even after they've left.

street corner,
street sign.
foyer
staircase
above bed,
flowers.

home full of ghosts.
maybe that's why
I've avoided it.

six years.

you greet me at baggage claim.

i should've been more careful –

                                with who I let inside.

i don't wanna be Beyoncé in love.

it's raining.
3 AM and it's raining.

i should be asleep.

--

you never think the last time will be the last time.
or maybe,
we just don't know it's the last time until the hours after
the last time we were what we were set in.
until it's 3AM and raining.

i should be asleep.

--

it rained the day we met.
I only said hi because saying hi is what you do.
if I knew then
what I know now,
let's be honest,
I'd probably still say hi too.

i can't remember if it rained that morning.
maybe it was that night.
day and night are sort of the same thing,
right?
opposites that fit,
depend on each other,
all that jazz.

--

i was day.
you were night.

but somehow,
we both fit better in the in-between space of dusks and
dawns where we could be gray
even though the skies were hand spun cotton-candy
pinks,
purples,
blues.

i've carried you worlds.
I take you with me everywhere.

--

the sky was the color of cotton-candy that day too.
I remember waking up,
looking out the window at the sun rising over Table
Mountain,
sun committed to its eternal task of shining.

i thought of you,
I couldn't stop doing that.

--

running away,
running to,
what're we so afraid of?
getting close, pulling back –
cycles.

i knew Lemonade was a personal exercise in healing as
soon as I heard it.
JAY-Z cheating wasn't a new thing.
we knew about the miscarriages too.

why is it so easy to ignore a woman's pain?
justify a man's behavior?
I know you saw the 'Resentment' video.
don't you ever for a second get to thinking,
you're irreplaceable...

--

except,
what if,
you are?
irreplaceable.

sandcastle turned house on which to stand.
I can't,
what is it about you that I can't erase?
don't promise me anything.
they never work out that way.

--

fuck up a good thing...
if you let me.

let you?
I'm not sure if I let you
or you let me.
maybe,
we should leave each other be.

i'm never gonna treat you like I should,
doesn't tell me you can't
or
don't want to.

it tells me you just might not know how.

--

tools.
do you even want them though?

--

i should be asleep.
sunshine has come.

--

i could teach you...
I shouldn't have,
no?
yes,
want
to.

--

I don't wanna be Beyoncé in love.

or,
maybe,
I do?

red velvet.

i want a love that gives.
releases like cake leaving metal pan.
not all at once,
but in bits and peace's –
safe.

i want a love that gives.
it's okay if it's a little rough around the edges,
they make knives for that.
run around,
peel up,
pair down.
i want a love that gives.
rooted in the knowledge of receiving back.
like faith
and shake
out.
grounded.
rooted in the intimacy of that.

i want a love that gives.
mixed and mingled,
able-bodied
rotund.
stacked tall,
layered deep,
covered
recovered
covering.

i want a love that gives.

hand out for reception –
will you meet me there?

from the small of back,
aching feet,
tired eyes and spatula,
mixing bowl turning.

sunny.

functional.

let me know
when/if
you ever
want
to
be.

katie.

"i mean,
I'm not
a
simple
girl.

like –
what
do
you
want…

from
me?"

souvenirs.

i learned chemistry from my mother and my mother's
mother.
the art of keeping people even after they have gone,
being kept.

souvenirs.
wrap sheets full of the things people leave behind.
people left behind.
always being left,
rarely doing the leaving.

no,
instead of leaving
mixing.
cakes,
cookies
putting on weight.
baking delicacies for people and simply leaving them at
ones gate.
showing up,
even when you've been left.
keeping people
even after they've gone,
being kept.

my dad has two closets
still keeps clothes he can't wear.
a basement full of pictures of him with a full head of hair.

family vacations,
weddings,
births.

boxes full of memories,
because sometimes,
maybe,
displaying them hurts.

packing
moving
going away.
all of this shit has to come down off my walls,
it cannot stay.

"Gabby, why did you throw all your art away?"
"Because it doesn't fit who I am anymore Mom. Doesn't
fit who I want to be."
"Okay, but you still should have kept some of it,
you know,
for the memories."

i never learned how to throw things away.
not routinely.
not systematically.
not at the exact moment it was time to.
purging was reserved for spring cleaning
and before going back to school.

getting rid of things at the beginning of a season
or start of a new chapter.
never sure the protocol for disposing of something
outside those time parameters.

knowing something doesn't fit anymore,
but figuring sometime in the gym might make it right.
holding out hope that one day it will fit less tight.

fight less tight,
and maybe a bit loose.
but not just right,
for just right is only something to aspire to.

no,
I learned to look at things for their sentimental value.
value.
sentiment.
sentiment I wish I never had.
memories I don't regret making,
but would be glad to forget.

heart that won't stop aching.
leaking.
smelling in the street.

maybe I hold on to so much because I'm afraid if I give it
all away,
the smell of you,
feel of you,
taste of you,
touch of you,
will fade away too –
just like the memories do.

souvenirs.
a pack rat.
afraid to let go.

I keep people,
even after they have gone.

probably because,
it is I,
who wants to be kept.

sunny.

~~eight.~~ six.

why are you trying to disappear?

four-see.

coils.
I leave them everywhere.

little pieces of me,
reminders for you of where to find me.
that I was here –
that we mattered too.

breadcrumbs.
Goldilocks was one of my favorite books growing up.
sink,
floor,
couch,
pillow.
marking territory.

some women leave bobby pins
or earrings.
I leave my hair.
shed my armor for you.

                                        is that,
                              a straight strand?

            you could at least clean her up.

grammy's.

certain songs will always remind me of you.
moments shared,
songs I play on loop in my head(phones).

somehow,
all of my favorite songs became ones you told me about.

i wish we had listened to each other instead.

confident.

~~sure, but...~~
sure, and.

sunny.

the smell of the sheets.

i know how you sleep…
you could never say I didn't love you.

you're not
                    what keeps

                                        me up
at night

                                anymore –
                                    though.

tit for tat.

things I'm not doing with you anymore:

this.
that.

spring.

out of sight,
out of mind.
out of body,
out of mind.

looking down at myself,
wondering what's happening.
you ever watched yourself fall in love?

i have and it's an interesting sensation.

they say that you should rise in love,
but sometimes you can't help but fall.

fall.
fall.
fall.

what is it about fall?
she always brings me men I know I can't have,
but want to keep anyway.

lock and key.
throw away.
I always fall for her trap and under their spell.
like the leaves on the trees
they enchant me.
ever growing
ever changing
ever exposing.
different sides of themselves so you never feel like you've
got the whole story.

forced to stick around because you want the whole story.
let me tell you,
about when I fell in love.

it was a warm fall day,
as far as fall days go.
a day that made you feel good like a track by Masego.
that girl was wifeable,
but not yet a girlfriend
holding out hope that one day
she'd be visible again.

visible.
viable.
a relationship was possible.
as you went down the list and checked it twice,
it wasn't hard to see that everything lined up nice.
stimulating.
electric.
movements.
movements.
conversations.
gibberish.

i fell in love in the fall,
in a window sill above a basement that was occasionally
light filled.

fall,
fall.
me, men, and fall.
but nothing,
ever lasts till spring.

comfort.

comfort is no shoes, no shirt, no service because the need
for naps is real.
legs overlapped with backs turned or toes but nothing
else touching, so neither of us ever forgets the other is
there.
going straight to the fridge because we're past the point
of asking. "You want some food? really, that's it? i know
you can eat more than that."
getting used to your body heat.
bus rides, white ad-i-das shoes and forehead kisses.
makeshift splints.
football matches.
not always knowing how to cheer,
but showing up anyway.

taking vitamins because "I'm tryna be healthy" even
though we both know you're lying.
knowing everything happens for a reason but never
understanding why you couldn't be my good thing.
"Did you reach?" and "I don't like that you travel solo."
coming to the hospital and bringing Burger King because
the doctors starved me all day.
bringing cookies for your mom because there's no way I
could show up at Thanksgiving dinner empty handed.
worrying about being accepted, only to end up being
loved.
missing them as much as I miss you, me, we, us, together
sometimes.

bringing me food or going out to eat and not having to
worry about "Eating like a girl."
staying up till 3 AM talking about the world.
spending all day in bed enjoying each other's presence
and the intellectual stimulation of it all.
laughter where there should be sleeping.
never sleeping.
oh my God's and Holy Shit's.
all the moments that make up whatever the hell this thing
we're doing here is or isn't.

eating in bed at 2 AM from the same to-go box because
we're both about the "fat" life.
sleeping while the other works.
not sleeping as well without your body there to through
over mine.
thinking way too deep and only coming up for air to
share our thoughts.
thinking on things together.
"Where you at?"

"You home yet?"
leaving the towel as if it's holding my place, waiting for
me to come back and use it.
"You get so excited," and remembering you don't like
chocolate.
taking time and no waiis.
waking up early to make pancakes.
white chocolate after a bad day and medicine when sick.
tears on chests.
football jackets ruined.
it's 'all i'm asking for is ifs' and ties that span states,
places, countries and oceans.

sharing EPs.
vibing out.
going to church with my mom, without me by the way.
the way your uncle said, "She's smart. Keep her."
watching sports with your family on holidays.
the way our legs intertwine and we don't sleep so
delicately anymore.
sleep like we're trying too hard.
sleep like we'll break the other party involved.
"I've got the chicken."
Christmas gifts I still sleep with.

it's "You're not intimidating to those who are worthy,"
and keeping track of what you can and can't eat.
like and don't.
list me as your emergency contact.
"What are you allergic to?"
hoodies that somehow always fit just right, even after/if
we realized we weren't right anymore.
it's "I don't usually do this" and "Have you ever tried this
before?"
doing your best to leave your baggage at the door.
learning your pet peeves, turn on's, and favorite songs.
promises made and promises broken.
lies told and transgressions forgiven.
New Year's Eve kisses at parties i lied about attending.

unclenched muscles and collapsing both into and on-top
of each other.
thinking I'd marry you.

comfort is that space before or between intimacy.
when you're finally relaxing and feeling each other
enough to be yourselves.
bringing all of who you are to the table because you're
confident and comfortable with the other person seeing it
— seeing you too.

what I wish I knew at 21.

at 18,
i wish i knew you can't make homes out of human beings.
i wish someone had told me that.

at 21,
i wish i knew how to not only listen to,
but apply all the lessons I'd already learned.
i wish i knew how to pace myself – in life, love, and all
that other stuff.
i wish i knew that yes, my twenties are a defining decade,
but i've got a whole nine (seven) years left to make
something of them.
i wish i knew that the 20-something Mark Zuckerberg is
few and far between and it's okay for me to not be that.
i wish i knew that comparison is the thief of joy and social
media is just highlight reels.
their highlight reels.
my highlight reel.
i wish i knew that i'm not doing this time in my life
"wrong,"
i'm doing it differently.

at 21,
i wish i knew it's okay to not know exactly what comes
next as long as i trust that God and the Universe are
working towards my good.
i wish i knew i'm no good in transition so i could've
better prepared for the one i'm going through right now
at 22(23).
at 21, i wish i knew not to doubt my abilities and to stop
procrastinating where my dreams are concerned.

i wish i knew that "overnight successes" put in hours
upon hours and years upon years of work,
so truly i'm just getting started and i've got to pay my
dues.

at 21,
i wish i knew that the weight i put on when sad in the
winter,
the physical and emotional weight of it all won't last
forever.
that spring and summer will always come and melt away
the ice in my heart while warming my soul.
i wish i knew there is courage in letting people go.
that there are blessings in moving through life
unencumbered
and my freedom,
my range of motion is too important to wish away,
waste on,
or share with the first guy that comes along.

at 21,
i wish i knew water isn't thicker than blood,
so i've got to be careful who i make my family.

at 21,
i wish i knew never to make myself smaller for the
comfort of other people.

but mostly,
i wish i knew how to snap back into form,
to normal size
when and if i did shrink down.
i wish i knew that anyone who asks that of me isn't for
me.

sunny.

at 21,
i wish i knew that the "out to lunch" feeling that keeps
me up at night,
would go away eventually.
that i will always come home to myself and to life.

because
unlike at 18,
at 21
i learned-
the only home i have,
the only home
i should
and can
call my own,
is always
within
myself.

a love letter to the girls who do, say, feel, give and are *TOO* much.

I could write the book on how loving people **too much** and too soon works out.
How loving people who lack the capacity to love you back works out.
How actively trying to not behave in lifeloveandallthatotherstuff like in manners past works out.

I could write the book because I am the girl that does, says, feels, and *gives* **too much.**

I'm dramatic and don't know what chill is or where to find it.
I often take up an extended residence in my head because it's easier to overthink, trust, love, hate, feel, fear, and live that way.
Safe.
In my head.
Where I am understood.

I used to wear my heart on my sleeve, but time has taught me to stop doing that.
So, now I wear a jacket and try to pretend that my natural way of being in the world is not what some would and have called crazy.
I wear a jacket because instead of writing *love on my arms*, the world has taught me the necessity of protecting myself –
protecting both you and I from me.

For, you see,
I am a girl that does, says, feels, *gives,* and is **too much.**
I don't know like, only love.
Don't understand dislike, not meant to be and didn't
work out.
There is only love and there is hate.
Even though,
as a person I'm always striving for **indifference** –
a calm, cool, collectedness that constantly alludes me.

I will give you the world,
my world,
your world,
our world,
before it is time
and way before you have earned it.

My love language is to give.
Give my time,
attention,
money,
affection,
love,
intelligence,
friendship,
laughter,
service,
soul,
spine
for and to you.
Because, my way of existing in the world assumes you will
give me these things back.
But, that is often,

not always,
never always,
where I,
where girls who are **too much** are wrong.

Wrong because the world can sometimes,
not all the time,
be cruel to women like us.
Wrong because people see our hearts and take advantage
of them.
Wrong because we give everything and did not think to
leave a breadcrumb for ourselves.
You know, so we could find our way home when our
giving gets us nowhere and everything has gone to shit.
Like it often,
not always,
never always does.

But still, we persevere.
Still, I persevere.
Put myself back together again and remind myself to be
more careful next time around.
And we are.
I am.
More careful.
At least, initially.

The problem is that *being guarded is not in my purview.*
It is not even a skill I can teach myself.
Trust me.
I have tried.
So, all I know and probably ever will is my leaking heart.
My heart leaking so strong they can smell it in the street.

A manifesto of sorts,
my leaking heart,
dedicated to my way of being.
Beckoning to both those I love
and those I love to hate.
Calling to those girls,
those other girls like me.
Offering myself as sacrifice.
Because, I will always be a girl who does, says, feels, *gives*,
and is **too much.**

Which means I will be a *giver* until the day I die.
Or until the day I close my windows,
lock my doors,
and burn my storage houses.

But, we all know that will never happen.
Right?

deliberate.

I could have seen you with my eyes closed and loved you
with no heart at all.

Deliberate. It's a choice.
Enigma. Wasn't going to make it easy.

That look in your eyes.
You got it when you were drunk, or silly, or being bossy.
It was equal parts mischievous and light.
Beckoning and pushing away.
But I always came.
Always,
all ways,
came.

You were like cruising down the highway,
Windows down and sunroof open,
On a 72 degree day,
With a sky so perfect,
Only God could have hand painted it blue.

Traffic.
Cruising is only ever easy for a second.

"Whatchu know about this?"
A laying out of discographies over drinks I never asked
for at an hour when I would have rather been asleep.

There was something so beautiful about the way the
music soothed you.
Made you feel like who you were was okay.

Some songs I'd heard.
Others I hadn't,

But, I knew that dancing in the kitchen
and fake forcing you to kiss me to Carl Thomas was a
love language I'd never known before,
One I wasn't sure could last -
Was even being felt back.

Here comes that look again.
Except, I'm rapping this time because you're playing a
song I know.
And maybe this is just the storyteller in me,
She seems to always see deeper than necessary into
everything...
But, it felt like you were in awe of me.
Both surprised I knew all the words and also expectant.
Happy this was a something we could connect over.
A language we might be able to share.
A look that read,
"Who is this girl who has stolen my heart? I might could
maybe really fuck with her."

A moment.
A movement.
Behind.
Leaning in.
Rapping lyrics in my ear and sending every nerve in my
spine into a tailspin.

I knew then you could break me in a way no one else has.

Calculated.
A little cunning.
A lot afraid.
A man who "knows what he likes."

Oh how I wish you would let me in.
There are moments where you do,
And in the littlest of gestures I can tell that you have.
Eyes in a GroupMe and shit, my bad's.
"Are those yours?," and
"Isn't that a little obvious?"

If this ends, you might be a song I can't listen to anymore.
A pain I should've,
But couldn't possibly have ever prepared myself for.

repeat.

all the self-care I ever needed was sitting right there,
in the space in-between,
while the light beamed,
ultra-light beam,
and in that moment,
everything
really actually,
was everything.

mornings were our time in a way different from that of
the night.
there was more laughter and visions of the future.
conversations at a normal register.

I always woke up late.

night was ours too.
well,
really yours if I'm being honest.
alive.
live as if you had music notes running up and down your
spine.
couldn't help but put on a show,
jive,
jiving,
no shucking though,
cuz this was all you.
music was always that thing we'd come back to.

a laying out of discographies at an hour half-past 12.
4 AM in Philadelphia,
sometimes,
it felt like hell.

hell because I knew you would never let yourself be mine,
even though I was only falling faster,
and deeper,
with time.

I downloaded all the songs you played,
so I could make a playlist,
and play it whenever,
I wanted, to make myself feel worthless.

caught up in something I could never know was real.
going through the motions,
trying not to feel.

whispers.
chills.
I want you to be rough.

with my spirit though?
I wish you'd be less tough.
be less tough,
and a little more gentle.
more open.
a lot less fickle.

you were, a slick verse over a tight beat I never saw
coming.
a song I thought I wouldn't like,
a score I thought I could only hate.
a sheet of music I couldn't quite read,
yet,
never stopped playing.

Repeat.
Repeat.
Repeat.

lurk.

i watch for you.

media, social.

blocked.

we come back in little moments.
ease of settle in,
never out.
surrounded.

heart open,
me down,
I remember what you feel like.

you ever had –
felt
they
were
made,
for you?
parts a true match.

two becoming one
should be longer than
round 1, 2, 3.
wider than you.
deeper than me.

like,
touch my soul
then break it.
circle around you,
circle of me.
didn't work though.

like,
if he won't take my love
he'll take my
me.

"I just wanna make sure we're not gonna be parents."

make sure
we
won't
be…

oh you did that alright.

blocked.

right.

i write about us in the morning.
in the space before the sun has risen and given way to
reality over dreams.
we exist better there,

I think.

sandcastles.

your fears are none of my business.

sunny.

Mr. Big.

"combo of both."

pick a side.

_ ıties.

quiet.
they're the ones that hurt the most.
pills you swallow
and tell no one about.

pains you'd think they'd realize they're causing,
except –
you're not on their radar
like they're on yours.

personal embarrassments you can't dare speak of
for fear of what your shame will look like in the sun.

a million cross roads.
hundreds of turning points.

you'll ignore them until you can't anymore.

it's the pain we silently bear,
that speaks the loudest.

sunny.

pray.

i pray for the day I feel less consumed by you.

-     on open ended goodbyes.

chrono trigger.

your side of the bed.

impenetrable.

there's something beautiful about dawn.
the way it washes away all fears.
dissolves insecurities.

you can't hide from the sun,
it's eternal job is to shine.

leg,
slightly over
rubbing foot against mine.
handsome in the innocence.
those first hours of daylight work their magic every
time.

you always fell back asleep first leaving me plenty of
time to get lost in the depths of Instagram, Twitter,
and my thoughts on you.

sweat.
day —
break.
sunlight.
can't trust that.

it is what it is.
it was what it was.
and,
I'm hopeful that someday,

maybe
I'll be able to see the beauty in the finality of that.

expiration dates.
paradoxes.
constant.
eclipses,
eclipsing,
eclipsed.
fully.

if it's me, then it's only me.
but really,
if it's you,
then it's only you.

thoughtful,
yet not.
mine,
yet not.
considerate,
yet not.
dichotomies.

night is for all the words we wanted to say
but wouldn't dare.
looks that communicated it all.
ambivalence.
understanding and assurance at the same damn time.

insidious.

night time was for all our secrets.
personal,
integral,
intertwined.

your deep dark place has nothing on mine.

limbo.

do not bring them when they're not ready.
weary of the ways of the world
and unable to love.

when their heart is broken.
for I am too busy mending my own and cannot
possibly spare any needles or thread to close their
open seams.

do not bring them before it is my turn to go.
go,
for I am always leaving.
wandering.
exploring.

do not bring them when I am feeling adventurous
for that will not work out for either of us.
adventure will always win.

do not bring them when I am bored.
for boredom should never be solved through
someone else.

they should not come when I am busy.

first time.

i can enjoy myself

without you.

when.

what do you do
when the only safe place to say

"I
love
you,"

is in a poem?

the girl that got you through.

i was just the girl that got you through.
you know –
around,
over,
in-between whatever it was they did to you.
pieces they left you with.
pieces they left you in.

pieces of yourself you didn't recognize as your own.
needed identified for you.
glued back together.

only,
glue falls off,
falls apart,
falls.
so I sewed them.

you couldn't handle heavy machinery
so the use of my sewing machine was out.
no,
hand stitch – yes.
back together
into something the world would recognize again –
created you anew.

i was just the girl that got you through.
always getting people through,
getting people over.
I really should stop doing that.
needles and thread get to be expensive and somehow,
I always end up the party left in shreds.

i was just the girl that got you through.
saved you from yourself.
saved you from her, him, them.
brought you back,
love unconditional.

i was just the girl that got you through.
and I hoped,
no,
believed
you'd turn around and get me write back.
only life often,
never always
fails to work like that.

if I knew I was your
"get you through girl,"
maybe I could've been more prepared.
as if one can ever actually prepare for the ins and
outs,
outs and ins of life
and that thing called love,
its evil, twisted twin.

snuck up on,
surprise.
get you through.
girl –
look alive.
too little,
not too late.

problem now?
I'd really like it if you stayed.

screensavers.

the journey back to myself started with the changing
of my screensaver.
for 6 months, it was you.

well,
not exactly you.
it was
us,
we
you and me —
together.

although that too isn't completely accurate.

it was a representation of where I thought I wanted to
be. where I thought I belonged.

problem being,
there's no way I could be there when I was here and
being reminded of the loss of it all every time I
opened my phone was problematic to say the least.

i never knew how much words,
no
images mattered until I changed my screensaver away
from you.
how that simple act would begin my journey home.

i wonder if I left my screensaver what it was for those
6 months because I needed to still feel connected,
or because I was addicted to the pain.

pretty sure it was the latter,
not,
never,
the former.

but what do I know.

soul ties are such a bitch.

now I keep my screensaver more neutral.
more me,
less
you, me, we, us —
together.
here's not there's.
unless of course
there has nothing to do with you.

the journey back to myself started with the changing
of my screensaver.
i thought that meant I was over it,
but then,
I went and made it my Twitter header.

shows how much I know about falling out of love
with a person, place, and time.
right?

track 16.

i still want to send you music.

how I know,
I'm not over it.

love for my grandmother.

Somewhere along the way,
I bought into the lie that I wasn't enough.
The lie that I had to accept XYZ piece of bullshit in order
to prove my worth.
The lie that back and forth, hot and cold is just what
relationships in 2017 are made of.
The lie.
The lies.

Somewhere along the way,
I decided to make wanting what does not want me my
ministry.
Second only to my leaving of those that want to stay.
Leaving, pushing away –
whatever you want to call it.

Somewhere along the way,
I forgot everything I was taught about love and traded in
those lessons for the enervating ways of the world.
Ways that were never in my purview.

Dysfunction is something I picked up.
It wasn't something I was taught.
My parents have been married for 31 years.
My dad is present, available, supportive, and emotionally
involved in my and my mother's life.

So where did I learn to want men who do not want me?

My father once told me that his mother,
my grandmother,
from whom I take my middle name was a fixer.

She thought she could fix men.
Tried to fix his father
and his brother's father –
failing at saving both.
I never knew her
but I think she passed this trait along to me

with her name.

I wonder if she was a giver too.
If she struggled with confidence in her relationships yet
few other parts of her life,
when she had no reason to doubt her worth.
If this insecurity manifested itself as overcompensating
for their shortcomings and inability to step up to the plate
by taking on all of the weight.
If she had my uncle and father in hopes that babies would
make them stay.
If she too gave so many pieces of herself away.

I wonder if she knew better
and if she did,
why didn't she act that way?
Better?
Why don't I act better?

It's not like there weren't signs.
I might not have been sure,
but I had an inkling.
There's always an inkling.
Where did I learn to ignore my intuition?
To favor the rationalizations of my brain instead of
listening to the ever constant beat of my heart?
A beat that has never let me down or steered me wrong?

The sinking feeling that travels from heart's chamber to
the guts
attaching itself to every membrane possible,
infecting me with the knowledge that I was probably
screwing up.
nestling itself deep down in there,
in my gut.
Where did I learn to hide things from myself?
To bury them so deep inside?

I can never eat the day after a heartbreak.
I had a beef patty in the fridge.

You ever felt your heart break before?
It happens quickly.
One of those little imperceptible shifts in the universe
so you'll miss it if you aren't paying attention.
Sharp.
Leaves you breathless.

My lesson in love is actually a lesson in heartbreak.
One I should've learned a long time ago,
but only figured out in this current iteration.
I hope I learned it for my grandmother too –
I like to think I'm her reincarnation.

Dysfunction isn't love.

What would it look like if I had enough confidence in
myself to know that anyone who isn't sure,
isn't someone I should want around in the first place?

overrated (butterflies).

all sparks ever did was set me on fire.
and not in the sexy way.
not in the amorous way.

no, sparks set me on fire in the
burning everything in their wake way.
desecrating this life and this body
God and I created way.

sparks were no good.

i think we teach people a lot of wrong things about love.
like being nervous is good.
like being nauseous is good.
like being unable to breathe,
think,
or speak is good.
like it's not love if there are no butterflies.

show me dancing round kitchen
bare-faced and beautiful,
falling flat on non-existent ass,
get up.

show me shower together,
and nap that knows when you arose,
couch,
next to,
can't sleep without you.

sunny.

show me spirit sensing bad day from miles away
piece of head on chest
peace of head on chest.

show me scalp in need of greasing,
dandruff scratched.
bonnet forgotten,
thrown back on.
show me thought out.

self not afraid to be,
and I'll show you love.

call me by my name –

love,
loved,
lovely.

pillows.

i keep a pillow where you should be
just in case you decide to come home
tired, and need to sleep.

i somehow end up throwing my leg over it at night too.
but,
it's no substitute for you.

two sets to sleep with,
when all I really need now is one
hope to roll over to you,
my sun.

i still sleep straight.
my side, your side,
no sides,
won.

universe big enough for both of us,
yet finding way through craters left in wake.

awake,
awoke.
awakened my love to the reality that me and you were
never actually a we.

i kept a pillow
where I wanted you to be.
until I realized,
I'm tired and need to sleep.

caught myself whispering.
I still pray for you.

goodnight
night,
sleep tight
don't you dare let the bed bugs bite.

i've learned to sleep without you.

i keep extra pillows in my bed,
extra softness
extra safety
extra down –

me, finally
only,
surely,
securely
holding it down for me.

ower in the lines we draw.
push,
pull,
erase.
the boundaries we learned to make.

boundaries for you,
bounded by me.

choices.
you have to choose.
eventually…

what's understood gets explained.
lock and key,
door code
thrown away.

i'll forget your address eventually.
phone number too.
forget our services,
never quite able to forget you.

the lines I drew
you hated.
yet never rose to meet.
sand drawn,
battleship.
sides.

you letting me, let go of thee.
"aye, tell Gab she on that bullshit."

i love you in.

i love you in peace's of poems I haven't finished yet.
Which isn't to say I love you halfway.
No, I love you in pieces of peace that haven't found me
yet.
Pieces of peace of paradise lost.
Pieces of peace of paradise found.

i love you in rooftops and impromptu cookouts.
i loved you in music, essence, and stories exchanged.

night
day.
sun
moon.

i love you in only wanting the best for you.
even if,
that best has no space for me in it.

i may be lighter without you,
but who said I don't enjoy heavy things too?
heavy lifting.
heavy living
down to build,
down to work.

i don't wanna love you halfway.

and,
i don't trust easy,
but it gets less hard every time.

Benediction

sunny.

one last poem.

i,
forgive

i loved you,
ya know.

sunny.

we get the endings situations deserve.
and we were never good at goodbyes anyway.

put your records on.

sunny.

sunny.

Acknowledgements

To my parents, Keith and Jacqueline Hickmon, for modeling what love looks like. To Duanecia Evans, Ashley Hobbs, Morgan Daniels and Kiyla Monet, thank you for reading early drafts and offering feedback. To Damola Akintunde thank you for bringing my vision for visuals to life. To Brandon Dennis, Carlton Burrell, and Dominique Collins thank you for cheering me on and asking questions. To Katrice Mitchell without whom I would be a mess, thank you for thinking through every step of this with me. To Dilion Robinson, thank you for being my hype man. To Fred Greene, for being a mentor and friend, thank you for always breaking it down and constantly keeping it real. To Jakira Shaw, Ashley Johnson, Destiny McLennan, Kamille Harris, and Michael Caesar, thank you for (tough) loving me to another side of myself, listening, and being patient with me as I realized the light you saw inside of me was real – I only had to claim it as my own. To Cajay Jacobs, I would've never begun or finished this book if it wasn't for you.

To you, for being a beautiful enigma and my favorite place to wake up, a gift I'll always be glad I got to unwrap, thank you.

To every one I've ever loved and everywhere I've ever left, thank you.

ABOUT THE AUTHOR

Gabrielle Hickmon is a daughter, friend, traveler, scholar, writer and lover. An alumna of Cornell University and the University of Pennsylvania, *sunny.* is her first book. Gabrielle writes and rants often on her blog The Reign XY and you can keep up with her via social media @Gabgotti or GabrielleHickmon.com. She is from Michigan but lives all over the place. Gabrielle is constantly chasing the sun.

Made in the USA
Middletown, DE
25 September 2018